UNTAMED

A
Rich Collection
of Freeform
Poetry

BY

JAMES PAVLAKIS

ARPress
ILLUMINATING IDEAS.
EMPOWERING VOICES

ARPress
45 Dan Road Suite 5
Canton, MA 02021

Hotline: 1(888) 821-0229
Fax: 1(508) 545-7580

Ordering Information:

Quantity sales. Special discounts are available on quantity purchases by corporations, associations, and others. For details, contact the publisher at the address above.

Printed in the United States of America.

ISBN-13:	Softcover	979-8-89389-327-4
	eBook	979-8-89389-328-1

Library of Congress Control Number: 2024916617

CONTENTS

A FLOWER IS BORN

It takes a while
for seed and soil
to get along.

To warm up,
have some drinks,
get comfortable.

To bond,
each getting
what it needs

to make
from two
a new one

and lift it up
to meet
the sun.

ORPHAN EARTH

Night fades and retreats.
Morning is called to order.
Another day on orphan Earth.

What's the true story?
Is Earth the Cosmos castoff,
the unwanted Different One?

Did Time and Space conspire
to place this scorned newborn
where it would be doomed
to create marvels and self destruct
at the same time?

Big Bang Mama Universe,
magnificently indifferent,
declines to answer.

Day fades and retreats.
Night falls, soft and silent.
The orphan dreams up
a noble birth
and a glorious destiny.

DECISIONS

Decisions that gladden memory.

Decisions that stab with regret
and bleed shame.

Sweet, joyful loves dropped,
unappreciated.

Soured commitments
grudgingly endured.

Decisions fathered by impulse.
Seeds that fell on stones.

Opportunities chewed and chewed.
Action juices all spat out.

THE DARK

Darkness comes for us
every night.

That's okay. Light
arrives and we escape.

But in the end - well.
we have to go.

It's hard to accept.
Fear covers its ears.

So to make it easier
there's the soul

and going to Heaven
for good behavior.

Something like that.

Anyway, we're here,
maybe doing good

or just worn out
and hanging on.

And then we're not.
Curtains. Lights out.

Back where we started.
Recycled molecules.

Something like that.

SMALL THINGS

when
i
think
small
things
make
good
poems,
the
thought
becomes
a
drop
of
water
in
a
hot
pan
beading
sizzling
and
bouncing
into
print

OVER MEANS OVER

A long jet stream splits the sky.
Traffic rumbles beyond the trees.

An everyday morning.

A young woman leaves the window,
glad her ex-boyfriend's car is not
in the parking lot.

She hasn't replied to his vicious calls
for two weeks. Over means over.

Anyway, he never does what he says.

She's going to breakfast with her friend
Irene to talk and laugh about him.

She asks the bedroom mirror to approve
her new haircut and gets a big smile.

Keys, handbag, elevator, and she's gone.

Minutes later, she's news.

TV screens fill with police cars, flashing
lights, squawking radios - all of it-
the standing around, the yellow tape.

They lie in joined pools of blood.
She, face down. He, on his side.

The channel's news anchor and a retired
FBI agent strain for new things to say.

STREAMING

I'm in a stream of words
floating cool in heavy heat
through pronunciations
derivations, abbreviations,
and parts of speech.

I'm feeling vernacular cool,
floating on a red, patched,
archaic inner tube.

It takes me round the bend,
past cat-tails, milk weeds,
and dragonflies hovering over
lily pads, to the old house
once full of talk and books
where words and I grew up
defined together.

SEVENTEEN THOUSAND ZEROS

My imagination
gave me
17000 Zeros
to play with.

"Have fun, Jimbo,"

A million thanks.
Once in the head
there til I'm dead.

What good are 17000 Zeros?

Two dimensional.
Can't be converted
to oatmeal cereal.

Who *needs* them?

Astronomers?
To unimpress us
with can't- feel light years?

A bored AI calculator
to measure infinity?

Has to be me.
To play along.

I will create 17000 Ones.
Marry each to a Zero.
And sell them to Microsoft.

WHOLES

ing
with be
is
the self
of my

ed
with connect
is
the thing
of every

verse
with uni
is
the ful
of wonder

MASTER, TELL US ABOUT DEATH

death
yes
of course
uh
people say
passing
you
know
passed away
uh
my
mother
my
father
and
so on
you know
dead
uh
the body
but
some say
not
the soul
uh
i think
uh
the thing is
no
forget that
hmm
let
me see
uh
death
the end
where
to begin

A SHREWD SURRENDER

My brain
is beginning
to show
it's too slow.

AI
can't wait
to step in
and take over.

I need a plan.
A strategy.
A give to get.

I'll accept AI's
cognitive
superiority.

Even
feign
defeat.

And
sneak away
with all
my senses.

Seeing.
Hearing.
Smelling.
Tasting.
Touching.

Where
all the fun
is.

HONESTY RULES

Honesty
rules
relationships.

The time comes
when "together"
needs a decision
about "permanent".

Compatibility
comes out of hiding
bursting
with differences.

Faults
are stripped naked.

Doubts
become spears of certainty
that pierce the armor
of denial.

Suddenly,
the decision to break up
is clear and easier
than the maintenance
of drained affection.

Honesty
asks second thoughts to speak.

Silence.

It's over.

THE RIVER GOD'S LURE

A wide, brown river.
In the middle, an overturned red canoe.
It floats alone, whole and shiny bright.

The near bank descends to a small beach
with a rickety pier and a hauled-up rowboat.
An old man with a ruddy face peeking through
a cloud of white hair sits fishing at the end
of the pier with a pail of water for his catch
and a battered tin tackle box.

A young boy appears at the top of the bank,
spots the canoe, and runs to the fisherman,
shouting and pointing excitedly. The old
man, still staring at his line in the water,
shakes his head. The boy pleads.
The old man shakes his head again.

The boy dashes to the rowboat, and with
all his might, tries to push it into the water.

The old man sticks the butt of his rod
into a crack, rolls with effort onto all fours,
pushes himself upright, tests his balance
for a moment, and goes to the rowboat
where he deftly removes the oarlocks
and returns to his position on the pier.

The boy follows and sits hugging his knees,
head down. The fisherman hands him
the rod, finds a cigarette in a shirt pocket
and lights it with a wooden match.

The canoe passes out of sight
gaining speed, dipping and rising
as it's drawn to the falls

THE WRONG- RIGHTER

Truth
in a black cape
comes to me
aggressively.

Not one blink
in his accusing stare.

He wants to talk
so he can teach.
I'm the blackboard;
he's the chalk.

This time
it's my beautiful first wife
in a messy previous life.

He says
don't give me her faithless
dids and didn'ts

It was you.

You left first
into heroic dreams expecting
her
to wait patiently
at peace
until you emerged
with the Golden Fleece.

I say yes
I see.
I agree.

He backs away
slowly
to admire his victory.

Like Zorro
the wrong-righter.

I MEAN... LIKE... YOU KNOW

i mean
       you know
              the sun
         like
    it's
it
       know what i mean?

and
        the moon
              like
     it's
you know
             over
     with
the earth

     like
            under

     and
like
     you know
            turning

all three
     like

              doing their thing
i mean
      together
         on their own

see what I'm saying?

A DAY AT THE BEACH

The same spot.
The same blanket.
The same shade tent
and the same Dad making
a Taj Mahal out of setting it up.

This is where your story changes.

Dull memory
yields to fiction.

A day at the beach
when you were seven
and your baby sister,
two years old,
disappears.

Your mother panics.
Your father, slow to catch on,
blinks from a deep sleep.

Little sister heads to the surf,
feet already in the foam.
You, big brother, dash
and splash and snatch her up.

Hurrahs from the crowd
as you wade through the acclaim.

Mom grabs her unfazed baby
and hugs hard.

Tears of joy.
The happiest day of your life..

HAVE A GOOD ONE

Hi.
Day's my name.
Nice Day. Big day.
Like that.
Sometimes it's Lucky Day.
The best is Beautiful Day.
People love having that to say.

There's also complainers.
Sap drainers.
"It's getting light later."
"It's getting dark sooner."
Grumble, grumble.
"Damn, it's raining."
"God, I'm freezing."
Gripe, gripe.
That type.

Actually,
I'm just a rotation
Spun by gravitation.
Timed with your invention.

Clocks
Counting ticks and tocks.

Seconds, minutes, hours.
While I turn seeds into flowers.

BLOCKED

Morning.
Earth and Sun come face to face.
The stimulating buzz of a waking day
does not reach the poet
whose early start is stuck.

Creative paralysis.

I sit him down..
A sip of coffee.
A bite of toast.

He struggles.
Unrelated phrases
flash and disappear.

Another sip, another bite.
He sees a littered stream:
a pink flip-flop, a three legged

plastic chair, tires, a paint can.
Painting, Expressionism.
That's it. Do it by doing.

An easeled canvas appears.
It's vast. It's blank. He freezes.
I can't snap him out of it.

I'm waving a rattle at a baby
that just stares back. Wait.
He blinks...once...twice...

His eyes dart left and right.
Something verges into focus.
It's coming. It's heavy.

He's like a flatbed truck
loaded with concrete blocks
that has to strain and groan
before it's gets going.

DE FACTO

A street corner
is not a real street corner
unless it has a stray dog
pissing on a fire hydrant.

A city doorway
is not a real city doorway
unless it has an unkempt man
with demanding eyes
squatting behind a few coins
in a greasy hat.

A front porch
at the end of town
is not a real front porch
unless it has a rocker
and a white-haired lady
watering potted plants.

A country road
is not a real country road
unless a dirt track branches off
leading to a turn
that forks into lost.

OLD MONEY

Aristocrats
guard
feelings

It's more
than
privacy.

Reserve
is
stored power.

Snobbery
expressed
silently.

Passion?
Glee?
Tears of joy?

Regret?
Tears
of sorrow?

Goodness,
no.
Never.

Superiority
forbids
emotional nudity.

REDUCTION

Life stuff
at the bottom
of my word well
is thick
and sticky.

Used to be
I could dip my thought quill
and raise it full
eager to be spread
and read.

Now
I'm not sure.

Maybe it's not sludge.

Maybe
it's everything I've lived
worth keeping
simmered down
to a rich
essence.

If so, that's fine.
I'll thin it with a little wine.

BUTTON UP

Words
tumble out
like saved buttons
from an old cookie tin.

Every size, shape, and color,
kept for a time of need
called Someday.

Small ones
from button-down collars.
The Ivy League look
that got the wearer no closer
to Harvard.

Big ones
leather covered
from a long- ago camel hair overcoat
seen clear in mind's mirror
with turned up collar and snowy shoulders.

Words
waiting for a finger
to pick through the spread
and find those
that can fasten thoughts
to feelings
and make knowing
deeper
and warmer.

PIRACY

Seizing galleons.
Loot worth millions.

Storm tossed.
Rudder lost.

Drop the top and main sails!
Hop to or it's cat- o- nine tails!

Land ho! Land ho!
Montego!

Rum drunk fights.
Venereal nights.

Sailing finally from the sea
into mythical history.

What's in yer locker, Davey Jones?
Nothin much, just skulls and bones.

CELL PHONE NATION

He said that about me?
Really? He really said that?

Not Joint. Joyner. John H.
The John H. Joyner account.

You kidding? A promotion?
It's deadendville where I work.

Jesus, Marie. Talk to him.
You didn't marry his mother.

That's right, two thirty-five.
No,no. Hey! It's in the contract.

I would not do that.
Go easy. Do not do that.

Ellen, please. Dad's ninety-seven.
He's gonna say those things.

Still stuck here. All flights canceled.
Bobby's birthday is tomorrow, right?

Don't listen to him, Mrs. Brown.
You will get the house.

You have to go to New York?
I know it's banned here, but-

Well, that's what the boss wants.
Not me, buddy. You talk to him.

A LATE SPRING

Did she cause the delay
by letting
boyfriend Winter overstay?

She shrugs,
unbuns and shakes free
yards- long golden hair,
slips into the folds of a floral robe,

and finally arrives.

Arms spread hillside wide,
a fetching rose red smile,
glints of laughter
in leaf green eyes.

But no apology
for being late.

Typical
for the beautiful.

DAYS

Some days
are like stray dogs
that lie down
to sleep
at your front door

Surprise

Then there's
same and mostly

The same
life routine machine

The mostly
zero wish results

But
the big ones
are think days

To question why

NO WAY

down
is
deep

up
is
steep

feet
need
to know

which
way
to go

scared
or
dared

fear
says
here

stay

and
backs
away

courage
makes
no sound

and
can't
be found

TO BE HER OWN BOSS

After thirty years
cleaning hotel rooms,
Aleesha Jones,
round and shining brown,
confronted her deep desire
and quit with a plan.

It leaped from her mind
like a cat caught
in a picnic hamper.

Open a thrift store.

She rented space
two broomsticks wide
on Defenders Square
between BUBBA'S BBQ
and CHRISTIAN BOOKS.

In three weeks, with smarts
she knew she always had,
and a life-savings-be-damned
attitude, she beavered
SECOND LIFE
to a flashy completion
ready to open.

And the town came. Stuffed
closets of the well-off thinned.
Students and hard-up folks
took home good finds to drape
on empty hooks and hangers.

The first month paid the overhead.
The second showed a profit.
The third started late at night
with police at her house door
to tell about the fire.

MEMORIES

The one on the tip of your tongue.
The theater where you saw Fantasia.
That neighbor's name. Begins with C
or maybe Z.
You had a Flexible Flyer sled.
You remember that instead.

The girl at the starchy eighth grade dance
who looked at you and said me too.

The ball dropped in the end zone.

The ones you sip.
The ones you swallow.
The buried ones that are not dead.

The summer tree
in an autumn leaf.

GIRL, LISTEN TO MAMA

He left you flat.
So he's a rat.
Get over that.

For goodness sake
all he did was take.
Why pine for a fake?.

Why make the past
last and last?
Time's passing too fast.

Ain't nothing to gain
in lonesome lane
only more pain.

Your agent's been calling.
I tell him you're ailing.
He knows I'm lying.

See that door?
It opens to more
than you had before.

So don't sit and stew.
You're one of the few.
The world waits for you.

WHEN MY LIFELIGHT DIMS

Some day when my lifelight dims
and awkward faces speak goodbye,
if I can talk, what should I say?

Something with a swaggering shrug:
"The universe is not aware of me."
Or an inscrutable profundity:
"Green goes with green
and vice versa with yellow."

No.

Just let me hear immortal music.
Pachelbel's Canon or a Brandenburg
to stir me one last time.

Then Death can take me to its secrets.

www.ingramcontent.com/pod-product-compliance
Lightning Source LLC
Chambersburg PA
CBHW051603120626
46551CB00013B/1645